America's First Serial Killers

A BIOGRAPHY OF THE HARPE BROTHERS

MURDER AND MAYHEM SERIES #1

WALLACE EDWARDS

Absolute Crime Press
ANAHEIM, CALIFORNIA

Copyright © 2020 by Golgotha Press, Inc.

All rights reserved. No part of this publication may be reproduced, distributed or transmitted in any form or by any means, including photocopying, recording, or other electronic or mechanical methods, without the prior written permission of the publisher, except in the case of brief quotations embodied in critical reviews and certain other noncommercial uses permitted by copyright law.

Limited Liability / Disclaimer of Warranty. While best efforts have been used in preparing this book, the author and publishers make no representations or warranties of any kind and assume no liabilities of any kind with respect to accuracy or completeness of the content and specifically the author nor publisher shall be held liable or responsible to any person or entity with respect to any loss or incidental or consequential damages caused or alleged to have been caused, directly, or indirectly without limitations, by the information or programs contained herein. Furthermore, readers should be aware that the Internet sites listed in this work may have changed or disappeared. This work is sold with the understanding that the advice inside may not be suitable in every situation.

Trademarks. Where trademarks are used in this book this infers no endorsement or any affiliation with this book. Any trademarks (including, but not limiting to, screenshots) used in this book are solely used for editorial and educational purposes.

ABSOLUTE CRIME

www.AbsoluteCrime.com

TABLE OF CONTENTS

About Absolute Crime.. 9

Prologue.. 12

The Violence Escalates 33

The Bodies Pile Up 53

Big Harpe Meets His End... 73

Little Harpe Takes a Head and Looses His Own... 82

The Later Life of the Harpe Wives............................ 92

Bibliography 97

Ready for More?... 100

Newsletter Offer 106

About Absolute Crime

Absolute Crime publishes only the best true crime literature. Our focus is on the crimes that you've probably never heard of, but you are fascinated to read more about. With each engaging and gripping story, we try to let readers relive moments in history that some people have tried to forget.

Remember, our books are not meant for the faint at heart. We don't hold back--if a crime is bloody, we let the words splatter across the page so you can experience the crime in the most horrifying way!

If you enjoy this book, please visit our homepage (www.AbsoluteCrime.com) to see other books we offer; if you have any feedback, we'd love to hear from you!

Sign up for our mailing list, and we'll send you out a free true crime book!

http://www.absolutecrime.com/newsletter

Prologue

Along the trails, on the farms and in the towns of Kentucky and Tennessee, a slew of mutilated bodies marked the travels of the Harpe brothers. The shocking discoveries of corpses of the innocent in the early years of the Republic threw terror into the hearts of townsmen and frontiersmen alike. The depraved Harpes left a revolting legacy - a blotch on the optimistic times when a new nation was being forged.

Frontiersmen, settling west of the Appalachians in what is now Tennessee and Kentucky, faced incredible hardships. Carving a patch of farmland from the dense forest, building a log cabin, and blazing trails to the nearest little community was hard enough, but the enterprise was made even more difficult by marauding bands of predatory bandits and unpacified natives.

We believe that frontiersmen in the new republic were a single-minded, hardy, honest, hardworking and heroic lot. They were, according to our romantic ideals, attentive husbands, good fathers and praiseworthy advocates of American values. The archetypical heroes of early America, Daniel Boone and Davey Crockett, stand as examples of the kind of men who selflessly rose to the challenges of the new frontier. Their blameless lives and exploits, first the subject of immensely popular biographies and fictional adventures, and later, broadcast everywhere through film and television, have obscured the reality of post-revolutionary life west of the Appalachians. Many, if not most of the frontiersmen, in the towns and wilderness lived lives that were, in the words of the Scottish philosopher Thomas Hobbes, "solitary, poor, nasty, brutish and short." Daniel Boone and Davey Crockett were exceptions to the rule.

There were two men on the frontier who lived the nastiest and most brutal of lives. Micajah Harp (or Harpe, known as Big Harpe), and Wiley (or Little Harpe), go down in the annals of America as being two of the most amoral, revolting and unrepentant homicidal creatures to haunt the frontier. They claimed to be brothers. They didn't look alike but both were completely identical in their total absence of conscience. They behaved about as close to animals as is possible for a human being. In the wake of their wanderings around Kentucky, Tennessee and southern Illinois they left a trail of dread among frontier families. This was a remarkable accomplishment. The region was continually wracked by rape, pillage and thievery, and the populace was used to the depredations of outlaws and outcast Indians. With almost no civil law enforcement the inhabitants were accustomed to dealing with criminal activity. They watched each other's farms, travelled in groups and exercised vigilante justice when the need arose. Of the criminals on the frontier the vile Harpe brothers were the worst of a very bad, large bunch of outlaws.

At one point in their career the two were part of a gang of pirates who plied their trade at Cave-In-Rock on the banks of the Ohio River in southern Illinois. The river was a busy waterway on which traders transported goods from Pennsylvania and Illinois south to the Mississippi, and families migrated with their earthly possessions to pursue their fortune on the frontier. The Cave-In-Rock pirates attacked the passing flatboats, scared off or murdered their occupants and appropriated their cargo.

In the spring of 1799 one of the flatboats came ashore upriver from Cave-In-Rock. A couple disembarked, climbed up a cliff and seated themselves on the rock to enjoy the view. The sweethearts held hands and whispered to each other their observations on the magnificence of the surroundings. It was their misfortune to be observed by the Harpe brothers, who were skulking in the woods. The two men stealthily approached the couple from behind and, breaking out in loud laughter, shoved them off the ledge and watched their bodies smash on the rocks below. When they told their fellow pirates what they had done, the homicidal pranksters received only muted praise for their exploit. The pirates were immune to the thrill of violence as they were well-practiced in the various ways of dispatching boatmen.

Not long after this failed attempt to get attention, Big and Little Harpe tried again to raise their status among their colleagues. Three men were captured in a battle over a flatboat and its cargo. They were taken to the pirate's lair and presumably trussed up to await their fate. One of the prisoners was spirited away by the Harpe brothers who stripped him and tied him to the back of a horse. They led the horse up to the top of the cliff over the cave and blindfolded it. They smacked its rump with sticks forcing the horse to the edge of the precipice where its flailing hooves dislodged some rocks. The gang below, hearing boulders tumbling down at the mouth of the cave, went out to see what was happening. They came into the open just as the horse with its naked passenger tumbled through the air and splattered on the limestone boulders at riverside. Up above on the cliff's edge Big and Little Harpe cheered and doubled up with laughter. This was too much for their companions. Rather than being suitably impressed by the murder, the pirates were stunned by the cruelty which was, even by their standards, shocking. One can assume it was fear of having what we today would call psychopaths in their midst that caused the outlaws to expel the Harpe brothers from Cave-In-Rock.

Where these vile men came from and even who they were, is unclear. The many versions of their story are not unanimous in speculation on their place of birth and their early lives. The two may not have been named Harpe at all, as they habitually used aliases in their criminal careers. But if they really were Harpes it is likely they came from North Carolina or Virginia and were born with the name lacking its terminal "e". In the days of rampant illiteracy and free-wheeling spelling it is likely that the "e" was added somewhere along the line and it stuck.

The Harpe boys were likely not brothers but rather first cousins. It is believed that they were the sons of Scottish immigrants William and

John Harpe, who settled in North Carolina. The son of John Harpe, Micajah was born in the 1760s. Two years later William Harpe was blessed with a son he named Wiley. The young Harpe cousins on the outbreak of the War of Independence joined one of the Tory gangs attacking the property and families of the rebels. Killing, stealing, murdering and burning were their stock in trade. In the chaos of war they helped themselves to the property of American patriots under the guise of furthering the King's cause, but their rape and pillage was motivated less by political persuasion than by greed and the pleasure afforded by violence. The Harpes were observed fighting alongside the British regular forces and militia in the battles at Blackstock's farm and King's Mountain in 1780, and at Cowpens the following year.

At the end of the War of Independence, with the British surrender at Yorktown in 1781, the Harpes, along with large numbers of loyalists and allied Cherokees, were pushed over the Appalachians into Tennessee. On the frontier they continued fighting joining the Cherokees raiding the farms of Patriots and their settlements. Sometimes the renegades were spectacularly successful, such as at the Battle of Blue Licks in Kentucky, where the Harpes, with Loyalists and Indians, defeated a force of 182 Patriot militiamen. The Patriot settlers strengthened their forces and forced the raiders to retreat to the Chickamauga Cherokee and Creek Indian village of Nickajack in the Southwest Territory that became the state of Tennessee in 1796. From this settlement the Harpes accompanied the natives on their periodic expeditions to pillaging farms. It is likely that the Harpe brothers were prime culprits in rape and murder. On one of their raids the boys kidnapped Susan Wood, who was said to have been rather ugly, and Maria or Betsey Davidson, described more generously as rather handsome. Big Harpe adopted these captives as his wives. The Harpe brothers parted company with the Cherokees on the eve of the destruction of Nickajack by forces of the Southwest Territory in September of 1794. Big and Little Harpe, with Big Harpe's two wives, moved to Knoxville.

This frontier town was a good choice because it offered a perfect environment for wild men like the Harpes. A visitor in the late 18th century described the capital of the soon to be new state of Tennessee as wild and unruly, dirty and disorganized. It was a sin city if ever there was one. The male inhabitants, much to the disgust of one reporter, even on Sunday caroused drunkenly in the muddy streets, swore profusely, danced and gambled openly and, without shame of promiscuity, swarmed the plentiful brothels. It was said around town that the Devil, old and worn out, had given up travelling and settled in Knoxville so that he could spend his declining years with like-minded people.

    The Harpe family cleared a piece of land about 8 miles from town in the summer of 1795. They built a log cabin, a corral for horses and put a couple of acres under cultivation. This was intended to be a front for Big and Little Harpe, who were not cut out to be farmers. They preferred the adrenalin rush of stealing and the satisfaction of living off the toil of others. On every visit to Knoxville, so it was reported, they had more and more pork, mutton and horses to sell to finance their non-stop carousing. Unconcerned with disguising their nefarious ways they came under suspicion, although nothing could be proved. A spate of fires destroyed houses and stables in the area and fingers were pointed at the Harpes, but evidence linking them with what everyone knew to be arson was lacking. The stables of the U.S. War Department's Indian Agent were set alight and when the residents rushed to put it out, the Harpes ran into town and attempted, but failed, to rob the home of the first Governor of Tennessee, John Sevier.

Little Harpe, like his brother, was adept at feigning innocence and exhibiting civil behavior when necessary. He courted and married on June 1 1797 Sarah or Sally Rice. How he managed to win the heart of the pretty and delicate daughter of a nearby farmer is unrecorded. Judging from descriptions of his wild appearance and unkempt nature one can only conclude that standards for potential husbands were very low at that time in the frontier.

The Harpes' idyllic life of thieving, gambling, drinking and womanizing came to an abrupt end in late 1798. A farmer by the name of Edward Thiel discovered that some of his horses were missing. He raised a gang of vigilantes from among his neighbours and headed off to the Harpe homestead where they found the farm abandoned. The Harpes, who always seemed to have prior information of any hostile raid, had packed up and departed. There were traces that Thiel's horses had been in the corral, so the posse picked up the Harpes' trail and followed it up into the Cumberland Mountains. They eventually overtook the Harpe brothers leading the missing horses. The two thieves were bound and led along the trail back to Knoxville. Just 5 miles from town the captives untied themselves and galloped off into the wilderness. With his horses in tow, Thiel, satisfied with the day's work, returned home while the Harpes made their way through the forest to what the locals called Hughe's Rowdy Groggery, located a few miles from Knoxville. They settled down to a drinking bout with the only other patron of the inn, a man called Johnson. His enjoyment of their companionship was short-lived. The following week Johnson's body was found floating in the Holstein River. He had been disembowelled, with rocks placed inside his corpse to sink it to the bottom. They had tumbled out as the current rolled his corpse along the riverbed. Hughes, the innkeeper, was identified as one of the last persons to see Johnson, and in spite of vehemently claiming that the Harpes were responsible for the murder, was severely beaten and kicked out of the county by some of his righteous neighbours.

Johnson was the first widely reported victim of the Harpes. They had wetted their appetite for slaughter in battle and certainly left civilian corpses here and there in Virginia, Tennessee and Kentucky, but these homicides were not laid at their door.

The actual count of the victims of the Harpes' campaign of homicide would never be known. The discovery of bodies and the record of disappearances in the sparsely populated backwoods of Kentucky and Tennessee in post-Revolutionary times were recorded haphazardly. Life was difficult on the frontier. Men would disappear, abandoning their families by simply walking off into the wilderness or heading across the Mississippi into Spanish territories. Others disappeared in the forest and drowned, starved or froze to death. Reporting a death to authorities often meant that surviving family members or neighbours would have to walk or ride long distances through tracts of forest that could harbor outlaws, Indians and dangerous wild animals. Official reports to the Sherriff at a county seat or to the few permanently resident churchmen were rare. So a count of the Harpes victims can only be approximate. As we shall see many of the corpses of their victims were discovered by accident.

On the basis of firm evidence the Harpe brothers killed 25 people, but some have estimated the number of their victims may have exceeded 50. This puts them in the same league as Ted Bundy, who is credited with more than 36 murders of women in the 1970's, and his contemporary John Wayne Gacy, who killed more than 34 young men. For these two, the gender of the victims is evidence of motive but for the Harpes gender, age and race were of no concern whatsoever.

They were indiscriminate murderers dispatching people they came across by chance with complete abandon. Their crimes were for the most part devoid of any detectable motive.

Modern serial killers are often motivated by a game of hide-and-seek with law enforcement. The Harpe brothers derived little pleasure from eluding capture because news of any of their atrocities travelled very slowly.

Skimpy reports of their murders in the few newspapers that had limited circulation on the frontier would not likely have fallen into their hands.

News of their violent acts was passed by gossip and rumor, and as a consequence was inaccurate. Hearing tales exaggerating their savagery may have spurred them on to commit even more barbarous acts.

[1]

THE VIOLENCE ESCALATES

The route west over the Appalachians from Virginia was a winding trail through the wilderness of Cumberland Gap. Blazed in 1776 by Daniel Boone, this path was travelled by missionaries intent on spreading the gospel on the frontier, displaced Virginia farmers (many of them loyalists), bold commercial entrepreneurs, and outlaws, misfits and adventurers. Having escaped their captors and killed Johnson near Knoxville, the Harpe brothers collected their wives, who were hiding in the woods, stole more horses and made their way to the Gap, arriving in December 1798.

One of the few victims of the Harpes who survived to tell about an encounter with them was a Methodist preacher named Lambuth. Crossing the Gap alone he was awakened in his camp by his spooked horse and suddenly attacked by Big Harpe. His assailant demanded his money and the horse. Going through the preacher's belongings the elder Harpe found a bible. He opened it and inspected the flyleaf on which the minister had written down a quote from George Washington.

"That is a brave and good man, but a mighty rebel against the King!" said Big Harpe. "This here bible mean you're a man of the cloth?"

The preacher nodded. Harpe then headed off into the woods but just beyond the light of the fire he announced proudly, "We are the Harpes." Later when the magnitude of the evil in their hearts was a matter of public knowledge, the preacher periodically told his congregation the story of his miraculous escape from the wicked killers.

The next victim of the Harpes wasn't so lucky. They came across a peddler named Peyton who was unwisely travelling alone. They murdered him and took his horse and some of his goods. Following the trail known as Boone's Trace into what is now Kentucky, they encountered two men from Maryland named Paca and Bates and without so much as exchanging pleasantries attacked them. Bates was killed instantly as a musket ball tore into his heart. Paca was wounded and fell to the ground. As he was attempting to get up, Big Harpe split his head open with a tomahawk.

A little further on near the hamlet of Crab Orchard the Harpe family stopped at a public house operated by John Farris. The only other guest that night was Thomas Langford from Virginia. Because the trail was so dangerous it was the custom for single travellers to wait at an inn for others to arrive and join them, under the assumption that there was safety in numbers. At breakfast Langford, touched by the bedraggled state of the Harpe party, offered to buy them breakfast. As he was settling up with the innkeeper he unwisely revealed that he had a bag of silver.

A couple of days later a couple of drovers were moving their herd along the trail near Crab Orchard when the cattle came to an abrupt stop, refused to move forward and then dispersed into the woods beside the path. The drovers explored the forest to locate what had caused their animals to balk. They found a bloody body tucked behind a log and covered with leaves. They hailed a couple of travellers and the four men carried the corpse to Ferris Inn, where it was identified as Langford. The Sherriff of the nearby town of Stanford was summoned and on being told by the inn keeper and his wife that Langford and the party of Harpes had set out on the trail together, quickly assembled a posse and set off in pursuit of the suspected murderers. The Harpes, making no attempt to conceal themselves, were soon apprehended and on Christmas Day they were escorted to the jail at Stanford, a town with a population of 200. Incarcerated in the two room log cabin jail the Harpes, under interrogation, said that their last name was Roberts.

On January 4, 1799 the five detainees were taken from the jail to the adjacent court house, also a modest log cabin. Three judges of the Court of Quarter Sessions heard the case in which the two men and three women were charged with "feloniously and with malice aforethought murdering and robbing a certain Thomas Langford on Wednesday 12th Day of December." Five witnesses were called. Sheriff Ballenger related the details of the pursuit of the criminals and said that he found on them a pocket book inscribed with the name Thomas Langford, clothing identified as belonging to Langford and a Free Mason's apron. The clothing was examined by Jane Farris, the wife of the innkeeper, who had a good eye for detail. She declared that she was certain that she had seen Langford wearing the jacket and pants exhibited as evidence.

The most damning testimony against the Harpes came from one David Irby, who said that he had travelled with Langford for five days prior to going separate ways. It was, he told the court, Langford's habit to enter into his account book all the expenses they incurred on their journey so that the costs could be fairly split between the two. He testified that he saw Langford write in the costs of a half bushel of oats and cheese that they had bought and the payment to a ferryman. The little black pocket book found on the Harpes had these precisely described entries. Further, said Irby, on hearing that Langford had been murdered, he went to the Lincoln County coroner and obtained a license to exhume the body. With the gravedigger Abraham Anthony he dug up the corpse, examined the face, looked in the mouth for an absent tooth and concluded that this was indeed Thomas Langford.

The judges found that there was sufficient evidence to bind the five prisoners over for trial at the April Term of the District Court. The day after the hearing the prisoners were taken by horse-cart to Danville some 10 miles away. The facilities for justice in Danville were only marginally better than those in Crab Orchard. The jailer, John Biegler, immediately bought a couple of horse locks to chain the two males to the floor and a new lock for the front door. His expense claim also lists three pounds of nails that were used to further secure his primitive prison. Four men were hired to act as guards and they served rotating shifts two at a time.

The Harpe brothers had taken breathers from their blood-lust on their travels from Knoxville. Rest and recuperation in their encampments included fire-side tussles with their women. As a result the expenses for the Danville jailer mounted. The female inmates were all well along in pregnancy. Maria Davidson Harpe (alias Betsey Walker) gave birth to a son on February 7 and Susan Harpe gave birth to a daughter on March 6. The cost of their midwives and extra rations of sugar, tea and whiskey were registered in Biegler's account book. However some relief in the expense side of the ledger came with the escape of Big and Little Harpe on March 16. The two managed to cut a hole through the jailhouse wall and flee into the countryside, leaving their wives and two infants behind. It was soon rumored about town that they had been assisted in their break out by the jailer John Biegler. He later quit his job and, as some said, used the bribe he had received to purchase land to begin life as a wealthy farmer. The savings in the costs of food at the jailhouse by two fifths were soon wiped out as Sally Rice Harpe required extra tea, sugar and ginger plus a midwife to deliver a son on February 8.

On April 15, 1799 Susan Wood Harpe, under the alias Susanna Roberts, appeared before the judges and pleaded not guilty. Two days later she was found guilty by a jury. On the 18th a new jury was empanelled and they found Betsey Walker not guilty. The court then dropped the case against Sally Rice Harpe and she was acquitted. The next day Susan Harpe launched an appeal of the guilty verdict and the Attorney General decided to place before the court a writ of nolle prosequi, or do not prosecute.

The freed women were returned to the jail to stay with their infants in the unguarded and unlocked facility. The Harpe wives said that all they wanted to do now was to return to Knoxville and live a normal life. Touched by this declaration the compassionate Danville townsfolk collected used clothes for the pathetic women and blankets for the swaddled newborns. An old mare was procured for a pack animal. With bundles of clothing slung over their backs, children under their arms and leading the mare piled with sacks of food, the women were escorted out of town by the jailer. He showed them the road to Crab Orchard where they would turn off and head south on their trek back to Tennessee.

Just 30 miles out from Danville the Harpe wives changed direction. The wily women traded their horse for a canoe and set out with their supplies and babies to paddle down the Green River.

The escape of the Harpe brothers became particularly galling to the authorities in Kentucky as just after their hasty departure from the Danville jail the bones of the Maryland travellers Pica and Bates were discovered just off the trail near Crab Orchard. An order was issued for the arrest of the fugitives and John Ballenger was given authorization by the Governor of Kentucky to pursue them if necessary into Tennessee and other states. But Ballanger was ahead of the game. On the trail he and his men came face to face with the Big and Little Harpe both on foot. Big Harpe, who was over six feet tall, of swarthy complexion and strong build, had piercing black eyes framed by matted long black hair. His shorter brother had cold blue eyes beneath a thatch of ginger hair. When the two parties met, Ballenger and his men were stared down by the glaring Harpes.

They hesitated and the fugitives took the opportunity to dash into the dense underbrush.

Before resuming the chase Ballanger went with one of his men, Henry Scaggs, to his farm and collected a pack of dogs. The hounds with noses to the ground led them to an impenetrable thicket of cane or bamboo. Several of Ballenger's men balked at forcing their horses into the mass of vegetation, begged off the hunt and went home.

Ballanger, in need of more men, rode off to a log-rolling going on nearby. He solicited help from a gang of men who were helping their neighbour move felled timber to the site of a cabin under construction. They all declined to join his posse, claiming that they had important work to do. At the same time Scaggs was also trying to recruit for the hunt. He went to the nearby farm of Colonel Daniel Trabue, who said that he could not leave home at the moment as he was awaiting the return of his son who was just off with his little dog at a neighbour's house to borrow some flour and seed beans. While Trabue was in the process of bidding Scraggs good luck in the chase the dog, beaten and bloody, appeared at his door. The two men swiftly mounted and raced to the neighbour's house where they were told that the boy had left hours before.

A frantic search of the woods between the two farms yielded evidence of that the fugitive Harpes had been in the area. An encampment was found with the carcass of a cow on the ground beside a pile of cold ashes. A large patch of hide had been stripped from the belly and two pairs of muddy moccasins with holes in the bottom lay nearby. The Harpe brothers had apparently whipped up new shoes to ease their escape on foot. Checking the footprints around the fire the searchers determined that only two men had been here. There was no sign that the boy was with them. This was a relief to their anxiety, but their reprieve from worry was not to last. The boy did not return home and a couple of days later Johnny Trabue's butchered remains were found by accident in a sinkhole.

Reports on the killings of the Maryland men and the Taube lad reached the office of the second Governor of Kentucky James Garrard. He issued a reward for the arrest of Big and Little Harpe of $300, at that time a huge sum roughly is equivalent to something like $50,000 today.

The Harpes eluded capture by Ballenger's posse and made their way north. In the woods near Bowling Green a man named Frederick Stump was fishing in a stream when he saw smoke curling up from a fire nearby. Thinking it was a sign that newcomers had come to settle next to his farm he went back to his cabin to fetch his violin and a plucked and gutted turkey he had prepared for dinner. Barefoot with the violin tucked under one arm, the turkey slung over his shoulder and a string of fish in hand, he walked across the stream to welcome his new neighbours. His thoughtful hospitality was misplaced, as unbeknownst to him the new neighbours were ungrateful murderers. Stump's body with his guts replaced by a few rocks was found by his friends a day or two later in the Barren River. The friends were immediately arrested but soon were released when it was concluded that the Harpes were the culprits. Their habit of sinking a disembowelled body with rocks was by then well known as a hallmark of the nefarious Harpes.

The two murderers made their way to the lower Green River and then down the Ohio River on to Cave-in-Rock in southern Illinois. How many they killed on this trek is unknown. No bodies were discovered in the region but that didn't mean that they were not engaged in their pursuit of death. A victim's corpse hauled off into the dense forest was soon disposed of by the abundant carnivorous animals. From evidence discovered by a wanderer at one campfire and footprints left in the soft mud surrounding it, it is quite likely that they did away with two or three men who were camping in the woods.

At this point no one was hot on their trail. Bellanger and his newly recruited posse, misreading the signs, headed south. The Harpes on their journey north evaded being caught up in a push to rid Kentucky of the plague of outlaws organized by Captain Young of Lexington. Young, known as "The Exterminator", lead a platoon of expert vigilantes in a sweep across Kentucky, killing bandits and outlaws and forcing many more to flee across the Ohio River into Illinois. Those bandits who escaped Young's dragnet walked, rode or floated down to Cave-In-Rock, a notorious bandit hideout. It was a crowded place when the Harpe brothers turned up at the mouth of the cave and asked to join the gang.

The Harpe wives and children somehow managed to canoe 200 miles down the Green River and then another 90 miles to Cave-In-Rock where, as planned in the Danville jail, they reunited with their husbands as one big happy family. The blissful reunion was cut short by the savage antics of Harpe brothers, who were more interested in murder than the income of piracy. There is, from time to time, a glimmer of honor among thieves. The maniacal Harpes, whose homicidal antics crossed the line even for a band of hardened pirates, were expelled from Cave-In-Rock.

[2]

THE BODIES PILE UP

Not suspecting that the Harpe brothers were likely to return to their old haunts, the residents of Knoxville were flummoxed by the murder of a farmer named Bradbury some 25 miles west of town. They soon however began to suspect that the scourge of the Harpes had returned to their community. The body of a young man, Isaac Coffey, was found just northwest of town on July 22. His brains were smeared over the trunk of a tree, which some thought was a ruse to lead them into believing that his horse had shied suddenly and crushed his skull. The more knowing Knoxvillians were of the opinion that if the Harpes were responsible they would certainly not cover up their work. It was not in their modus operandi to plant misleading evidence. In fact, the Harpe brothers' actions were never motivated by any desire to hide their crime. The appalling murder of Coffey was the work of uncalculating minds bent only on violence. The Harpes had indeed pulled the poor fellow off his horse and smashed him headfirst again and again into the tree.

The killing spree continued apace. Two days after the Coffey killing the body of William Ballard, cut open and filled with rocks, was found in a river. This was linked to the disposal of

Johnson's corpse more than a year before and confirmed that the Harpes were in fact back. Word spread quickly so there was not a person in the county who was not on the alert. But being aware of danger did not guarantee safety, as James and Robert Brassel found out. The brothers, making their way down a country path, James on foot and his brother ahead on horseback, were approached by two men who said that they were part of a posse looking for the Harpe brothers. They indicated that the rest of the party would come along shortly and invited the Brassels to join in the hunt. The two agreed, whereupon they were suddenly accused of being the Harpe brothers. One of the men relieved James Brassel of his musket and tossed it away, expertly tied him up and threw him on the ground. Robert Brassel jumped from his horse and tried to pick up his brother's gun. The shorter of the two villains instantly grabbed the weapon and pointed it at Robert. Seeing he could do nothing to help his brother Robert Brassel took off into the woods and managed to outrun his pursuer, whose identity was later confirmed to be Little Harpe to no one's surprise.

Brassel ran to get help. He recruited a small group of men and led them back to the spot where he and his brother had been assaulted. James was lying on the ground still trussed up. His body was a mass of wounds and his throat had been cut. The little band of men rode down the path in the direction they supposed that the perpetrators had fled. They were astonished to come face to face with Big and Little Harpe with their wives and children making their way back to the scene of the crime. The trembling horsemen murmured to each other that they should remain silent so as not to anger the Harpes and not make a move unless provoked. The two groups glared at each other and silently proceeded in opposite directions.

The Harpes did not hang around Knoxville for long. Soon their trail was picked up in Kentucky where the mutilated body of John Tully was discovered lying beside a wilderness path. When the people of Tennessee got news of the Tully killing they breathed sighs of relief. Terror spread among the Kentuckians. The reality of the danger was confirmed with the discovery of the bodies of new homesteader John Graves and his 13 year old son. Awaiting the arrival of the rest of the family they had constructed a cabin and outfitted it with the necessities for a pleasant domestic life. A neighbour arrived to bid them welcome and found the home silent and vacant. He hailed the new arrivals thinking that they might be in the woods. Led to explore the brush at the edge of the clearing by a flock of buzzards, he found Graves and his son with their heads split open and Graves' own bloody axe next to their corpses.

The bodies now mounted up quickly as the Harpes moved on to Russellville. Their route was marked by the corpses of a little girl and a black boy whose head had been repeatedly smashed into a tree. A little further on the Harpes encountered an encampment in the woods of the Trisword brothers, who were accompanied by their wives, several children and black servants. From the evidence at the site it was believed that the Harpes were joined by some Cherokees in killing the entire party with the exception of a man who escaped and ran for help. Attributing part of the slaughter to

Indians was the only way the people in the area could explain the carnage. But as we know, the Harpe brothers were quite capable of savagery exceeding even that portrayed in the most lurid and exaggerated accounts of Indian raids.

The Harpe clan camped in the woods each night and exercised some caution to avoid detection. They overestimated the courage of anyone or any group that were on their trail, for the terror they struck among the populace meant that everyone in Kentucky retreated at night behind barred doors with muskets close at hand. Big Harpe cautioned Betsey, Susan and Sarah that they must keep their infants quiet at night. Some later said that this was because he was afraid that their wails would reveal their location to pursuers. A more likely explanation for commanding the women to keep the babies quiet was Big Harpe's insistence on uninterrupted sleep. His two wives and Little Harpe's wife were, as they later said, in the habit of taking the children off into the forest a little way off so as not to bother the men. One night Big Harpe was woken by one of the babies crying. He pulled the offending infant from his mother's arms and, holding its heels, swung it against a tree, smashing its little head. He then tossed the dead baby into the bush. It is not sure whose child Big Harpe killed. Some, unable to believe that a man could do such a thing let alone to his own offspring, have concluded that it was Little Harpe's child. As there was no limit to either Harpe's behaviour it is just as likely that he killed his own daughter as his brother's son.

It is hard to believe that the Harpes, when they settled again in Kentucky near Henderson, were not recognized. Nevertheless in spite of the circulation of the Governor's warrant for their arrest and the offer of a very generous reward (to which was appended an accurate description of each of the men), they somehow managed to rent a little cabin in the woods near Canoe Creek close to Henderson. The area was more densely populated than other tracts of Kentucky. Settlers were drawn here by the many salt licks that yielded the mineral necessary for the raising of livestock, and preservation of food and cooking. On any day several frontiersmen could be seen travelling unprotected on forest trails on their way to and from the sources of salt. In the past they were harassed by outlaws but the raid by Captain Young of Lexington had succeeded, it was thought, in eradicating them. At least 15 had been killed and the rest forced across the Ohio River. Thus the frontiersmen around Henderson felt fairly secure and if they were aware of the Harpes trail of murder they believed that they were still in distant Knoxville or in southern Kentucky.

The first inkling that the region was not safe and that an escapee from Captain Young's dragnet was on the loose came with the murderous attack on John Slover as he was on his way to a salt lick. Fortunately for Slover he had considerable experience in moving quickly in the face of danger, having once been an Indian captive. As such, he would have found himself integrated into the band and put to use as warrior in their raids against other Indians and white settlers. Slover escaped his attackers and alerted the authorities, who put the new settlers in Canoe Creek under watch. The spies were detected by the Harpes. The women and children melted away into the forest and the

Harpe brothers took off on a trail heading south.

On August 21, 1799 they stopped at the home of James Tompkins on Deer Creek, where they convinced him that they were Methodist preachers. He kindly invited them in for supper and the meal commenced with Big Harpe reciting a long grace. In the course of mealtime conversation the guests asked Tompkins if he had been hunting lately. He said that he did not have any powder, so he had taken no deer lately. Big Harpe then produced his powder horn and poured out some of its contents, which he wrapped in paper and handed to Tompkins. After thanking Tompkins for his hospitality the Harpes said their farewells and rode off in the twilight to the neighbouring farm of Silas McBee.

The two men were presumably intent on killing McBee, a justice of the peace. They held a grudge against McBee it was said because he had cooperated with "The Exterminator" Captain Young in his raid on outlaws in the region. The Harpes rode through the forest and approached the clearing around McBee's house. They tied their horses to trees and stealthily worked their way into McBee's farm yard. Nearing the house they were attacked by McBee's dogs and fled. This much is known from what McBee later told his friends and the authorities. What happened next is based on stories told over and over again in the area. They are probably true in the broad strokes but likely tinged with fantasy in the details.

Riding away from McBee's the Harpe brothers headed west to the home of Moses Stegall. They knocked on the door and Moses' wife opened it. Recognizing the two faces illuminated by the light of a candle she said that her husband was not in. "He's off to Henderson and will not come back," she explained.

Big Harpe adopted a hang-dog look and said, "We're goin' home. Got caught by the dark. Little brother's damn horse looks to be pulling up lame."

"You can't stay here. The loft is taken by Mr. Love, the surveyor. He came by earlier with business for Moses," replied Mrs. Stegall.

"That makes no never matter to us. We'll just join him. Be up at dawn before he rises and be gone and no one the wiser," replied Big Harpe. "Let us in just like if Moses were here."

"All right but keep quiet or you'll wake the little one." Moses Stegall's wife held the candle aloft and led them around to the side of the house and pointed to the steps leading to the loft. "Up you go boys and be gone by dawn."

In the windowless and pitch dark loft the Harpes climbed into bed where Love was snoring loudly. "Jazus he's loud," said Little Harpe, "how we goin' to get any sleep with that goin' on."

Big Harpe rolled over to extract his knife from its sheath on his belt. He pulled it out slit Love's throat and said to his brother, "now that should do it. No more snorrin' from that bugger." The two nodded off and had a refreshing night's sleep.

The next morning they descended the staircase, went around to Stegall's front door and knocked gently. When Mrs. Stegall answered they asked if they could come in and have breakfast.

"You can come in," she said, "but there'll be no cookin' as the little one's all a dither about coughin' and wheezin'. I'z got to be attendin' him constantly the poor little mite just four month old and not fit for a day longer in this world."

Big Harpe put his hand on her shoulder. "Never you care," he assured her, "me and me brother will rock him while you get the fire goin' and cook some victuals. Love will be down soon and wantin' to eat too."

Mrs. Stegall lit the fire, splashed some water and oats into a pot and popped it on the stove. While she was stirring the gruel she looked over at the Harpes who were seated on either side of the cradle. "My youse boys is good at that," she said complementing them on their skill at quieting her baby. "Little fellow never give's up wailin' and flailin' no matter what I try."

"However you done that?" she asked as she stepped over to have a quick look at her silent baby. The blanket over the swaddled infant was pulled up over his face. She bent and tugged it down and saw that her infant son was quiet because his throat had been cut from ear to ear. Her hands flew up to her face and before the first wail made its way from her lungs to her gaping mouth Big Harpe had unsheathed his bloody knife and plunged it into her heart. Little Harpe followed his brother's lead and thrust his knife into her chest then stepped over to the table, grabbed a butchers knife and stuck it into the collapsed body of Mrs. Stegall. The brothers nonchalantly left the knives in the corpse. Later the discovery of three knives in what remained of the body suggested to some that the Harpes had been assisted in the murder by one of their wives.

After fortifying themselves with a bowl of gruel Big and Little Harpe collected handfuls of clothing, stuffed them in the stove and piled the cradle with the dead baby and a couple of chairs on top. They rounded up the dogs in the yard, threw them in the house and closed the door. Standing in the clearing they waited to see the flames engulf the cabin. On hearing the dogs yelping in pain Little Harpe said, "I reckon they smell hell." The two men then made off through the woods on fresh horses taken from Stegall's barn.

The first appearance in print of an extended description of the Harpe brothers career in murder was a report by James Hall in 1824. The crimes he described were so horrific that his story was declared untrue by a contemporary newspaper. It was only after he expanded his story in subsequent publications that it became clear that Hall had not made up the entire story. For him the three murders at Stegall's home and the killing of one of the Harpe babies was proof that what drove the Harpes to murder was not greed or any of the other usual motives for crime. They stole what would have been normally given to them freely and took from their victims only what they needed for immediate needs. They simply had a savage thirst for blood and killed without the motive of obtaining any benefit for themselves. In modern parlance, the Harpes were psychopaths and what is more indiscriminate and sadistic killers. One might ask what made them into such evil characters. Because they were related their psychopathy may have been genetic. Or they both may have suffered what we today call post traumatic stress syndrome. It was reported that Big Harpe said what drove them to murder was an intense dislike for all humanity. Their antisocial behaviour may have been incubated in the violence of the American Revolution.

[3]

Big Harpe Meets His End

With Stegall's house in flames incinerating three bodies, it is believed that the Harpes' plan, if indeed they had one, was to ambush McBee as he rushed down the trail to his neighbour's burning house. The evidence for this was the discovery later of the bodies of two men, Hudgens and Gilmore, lying on the trail between the two homesteads. Some said that the two on their way to a salt lick were approached by the Harpes and accused of burning Stegall's house. They were pulled off their horses, Hudgens was stabbed in the heart and Gilmore had his brains dashed out with the butt of his own gun. McBee avoided the ambush by taking a shortcut to Stegall's house. Unable to do anything about the smouldering ruins he alerted another neighbour, John Pyles, and they both took the shortcut back to McBee's house. It was not long after that Moses Stegall rode up and was told of the disaster.

More volunteers were raised and the next day a party of six vigilantes went out in pursuit of the Harpes. They came across two dead and mutilated dogs, which they recognized as belonging to Hudgens and Gilmore. Proceeding cautiously they saw an encampment where the Harpe brothers and their three wives were sitting around a fire. McBee put the spurs to his horse. As he thundered into the camp Big Harpe mounted and rode off in one direction and Little Harpe headed off into the bush on foot. McBee reigned in and, hearing a noise in the woods, levelled his musket and shot. He heard a cry and then a man stumbled out of the forest and fell. He was not one of the Harpes but a settler, George Smith, who had been lurking around after being scared out of his wits by an encounter with the homicidal brothers.

The vigilantes demanded that the women point out the direction Big Harpe had taken in his escape. Two men were left to guard the women and four others went after Big Harpe. When they overtook him about two miles from camp he reigned in his horse and pointed his musket at the heart of the lead pursuer, one John Leiper. He pulled the trigger but his gun didn't fire, so he flung it on the ground, pulled out his tomahawk and charged. Leiper, keeping his cool, aimed his musket and shot Big Harpe in the torso. Sagging in his saddle Harpe said that he was ready to surrender so his pursuers dismounted, at which point he kicked his horse and headed off again on the trail. He was soon overtaken a second time and pulled from his horse. Lying on the ground he begged for water, which McBee supplied by filling his shoe at a nearby creek. Harpe was, according to some reports, asked if he wanted to confess to his crimes but he responded that he only regretted killing his own son. Some said that he confessed to 20 murders. Pressed to explain his homicidal character, others reported he said that he had been badly treated and thus became disgusted with all mankind. It fell to Stegall, who had suffered the loss of his entire family, to hasten the exit of Big Harpe from the world. The reports of what happened next vary. Some said that Stegall pulled out his knife and slowly cut off Harpe's head while he was still alive. Others said that Stegall pointed his musket at Harpe, who wiggled his head to avoid the final bullet before being shot in the heart. Stegall's intent was to protect the head, which in this version of the tale he cut carefully off the dead man.

However Harpe lost his head, while still alive or when shot dead, the trophy was put in a sack and tied to a saddle and the vigilantes departed, leaving the murder's body to be consumed by animals. Three miles north of Dixon Harpe's head was installed in a tree at a crossroads where it remained as a warning to all outlaws of the fate they could expect. It was removed several years later by a superstitious woman who believed that the pulverized skull of an evil man like Harpe could cure a sick family member.

Not a trace of Little Harpe could be found in the forest near their final encampment. The women were taken with their babies and locked up in the little log jail at Henderson. They were remanded on September 4, 1799 on charges of being party to the murder of the Stegalls and two days later, under the protection of five guards, were transported to Russellville, the county seat. The pathetic state of the women roused the sympathy of the Sherriff of Logan County, Major William Stewart. He removed them from the jail, confined them in the courthouse, provided them with new clothes and brought them spinning wheels to pass the time while awaiting trial. Under threats by the populace to burn the courthouse and lynch the prisoners, Stewart removed the women and put them up in a secret place in the country.

The trials were set for the 29th and 30th days of October. Back in Dixon, Stegall, fuming with rage at what had happened, threatened to ride into Russellville and exact revenge if the women were declared innocent. He did not carry out his plan even when the three were found not guilty. At some point they told Sheriff Stewart that when they were joined by the Harpes after the killings at Stegall's house, Big Harpe proposed that the two remaining children be killed so that they would not hold up their flight. Little Harpe agreed but his wife ran off with the children just before the vigilantes arrived and the brothers fled the encampment.

The men who had killed Big Harpe and captured the women were rewarded for their efforts but some of them fell under suspicion by their neighbours. John Leiper, who apparently knew the Harpes, was thought to have colluded with them in their crimes. He was, until his death, looked upon with suspicion. Stegall was also thought to have been known to the Harpes. This was why, some said, his wife invited them to stay the night and why Stegall had silenced Big Harpe by swiftly cutting of his head. Stegall was murdered in 1806 by the two brothers of a girl he was thought to have raped. As life and justice on the frontier was nasty and brutish and guilt was determined outside of court by rumor and innuendo, it is impossible to say whether Stegall was a hero or villain. He certainly was not as nasty a piece of work as the Harpes.

[4]

Little Harpe Takes a Head and Looses His Own

In spite of a widespread search Little Harpe was not to be found. Nothing more was heard of him until 1804 when under the alias of John Setton he appeared in Natchez with the head of a notorious highwayman named Samuel Mason. Setton and a friend exhibited the carefully preserved head, split by a tomahawk, to crowds of the curious on the streets of Natchez. They brought it to the authorities and claimed the reward that had been offered for killing the outlaw. Unfortunately for them the treasury of Mississippi was depleted at the time and they were told to wait for payment.

The outlaw Samuel Mason, whose head Wiley Harpe so proudly showed around Natchez, had a career that paralleled that of the Harpes. He was by all accounts considerably less bloodthirsty than they were. Mason was born in Virginia in 1739 and served there as captain in the Patriot militia, surviving an Indian ambush in which all of his men were killed. Wounded in the skirmish he gave up his military career and moved to Pennsylvania, where he was elected justice of the peace and later even became an associate judge. Such occupations seem quite ironic when one considers

Mason's later exploits. He moved on to become a Kentucky frontiersman and after some years slogging away as a farmer in Henderson he moved down the Ohio River, building a home on Diamond Island where he began his career as a pirate. Like many of his gang he was a resentful veteran of the Revolution only able to thrive in the backcountry where the trappings of civilization were few and the opportunities for criminal activity were unlimited. Pulling up stakes again in 1797, Mason moved to Cave-In-Rock. There was a leadership vacuum in the pirate lair. The former gang leader was one Jim Wilson who cleverly put a sign at the mouth of the cave identifying it as "Wilson's Liquor Vault and House of Entertainment." The promise of diversion for flatboatmen worked wonderfully and either before or after the unwary traders partook of liquor or the entertainment they were robbed and murdered, or beaten up and released in the woods. Wilson was killed by one of his own men opening the way for Samuel Mason, former farmer and judge, to take over the operation. Mason refined the business by having men stationed on the banks of the river to offer their services as pilots to descending flatboats. The boats under the pilots' direction were run ashore and captured by other gang members. As another ruse Mason stationed women on Diamond Island upriver from Cave-In-Rock. They pleaded with the passing flatboatmen for a ride down to the cave. The traders got a lot less than they hoped for. The women, of course, persuaded the traders that they must wait for "entertainment" until they arrived at Cave-In-Rock. When they were put ashore they were attacked, robbed and in one unfortunate case driven naked on horseback over a cliff by two young men named Micajah and Wiley Harpe.

Mason, who stood out as a bit of a thinker among the crowd at Cave-In-Rock, soon hit on an idea for more profitable larceny. When the gang appropriated the cargo and flatboats of merchants plying the river they were faced with the problem of disposing of the appropriated goods. The pirates were delighted when they found cash on their victims and not so pleased to acquire industrial and agricultural goods. It required some effort to turn the cargo into money. The pirates had to navigate the stolen flatboats downriver, exposing themselves to other pirate's depredations, and then sell the cargo at points south along the Mississippi, then take the long return journey on horseback to Cave-In-Rock. Mason figured that he could up his income if he just sat in the woods adjacent to the 550 mile trail from Natchez to Nashville, known as the Natchez Trace, and pounce on retuning merchants and relieve them of their cash. So Mason packed his bags and moved his family south to reap the rewards of a highwayman on the Natchez Trace.

After a few years filling his pockets on the Trace, Mason settled his family on a farm near Caruthersville in Missouri, then under Spanish control. He secured a passport, giving him the right to live there but was absent a great deal of time, preferring the sweat-free occupation of pirate on the Mississippi. He was careful to carry out his thieving only in American territory. Sometime around 1802 Wiley Harpe joined the Mason gang. About the same time the Governor of the Mississippi Territory was supplied with enough evidence to issue a warrant and offer a reward for the arrest of the Mason gang for piracy. Mason, several gang members and his family were picked up by the Spanish authorities and taken to New Madrid for trial. He claimed that he was a simple farmer and that he had never contravened the laws of Spain. The large sum of $7,000 dollars in cash found in his home and 20 scalps suggested otherwise to the officers of the court. Mason, his cohorts and family were put aboard a riverboat and shipped off to New Orleans, where the Spanish handed them over to American authorities. While being transported up-river for trial in Natchez, Mason and his gang escaped custody. Not long after setting up camp ashore Wiley Harpe, known to the Spanish court and American law enforcers as John Setton, and a co-conspirator, John May, turned on Mason and split his skull with a tomahawk. They detached

Mason's head, preserved it in a ball of clay and took it by canoe up to Natchez.

Eventually the money was found in the territorial treasury to pay Setton and May their bounty. They were summoned to court and appeared before a judge with their claim. It was literally at the last moment before the signing of the order to pay the reward when a man rushed into court and called a halt to the proceedings. He had recognized horses in a stable and told the judge that he and his friend had been robbed on the Natchez Trace by the two claimants of the reward. Setton and May were clapped in irons and arrangements were made for their trial. One of the witnesses called at the proceedings was an individual who had testified at the Danville trial of the Harpes. He identified Setton as Little Harpe because he had a mole on his neck and two web toes. A second witness who identified Harpe was an individual who had been wounded by him near Knoxville. Jails on the frontier were not typically very secure and bribery of poorly paid guards was rampant. Not trusting that their protestations of innocence would ensure their freedom Harpe and May slipped out of the Natchez lock-up and headed up the Trace. They didn't enjoy their liberty for long. A posse caught up with them and they were escorted to Greenville for trial. Both were convicted of robbery and executed on February 8, 1804. Their heads, as was the custom, were stuck on poles and installed in separate places on the Natchez Trace as a warning to other outlaws.

[5]

THE LATER LIFE OF THE HARPE WIVES

Acquitted by the court in Russellville, Kentucky after the Stegall killings and the subsequent execution of Big Harpe, the three Harpe wives were released. Sally Rice Harpe returned to Knoxville to live with her father. After his death she moved to Illinois where she remarried a man who in the quaint language of the day was described as highly respectable. She had a large family.

Susan Wood Harpe settled in Russellville and lived, it is said, a normal life. Betsey Davidson Harpe continued to use her alias of Betsey Roberts. She remarried in 1823 and moved north to Illinois where she died in the 1860's. What happened to the two surviving Harpe children is unknown.

Why the Harpe brother's wives continued to follow their brutal husbands on their travels through Tennessee and Kentucky when they had plenty of opportunities to escape was of great interest to 19th century chroniclers of the Harpes. Their lives, following the consignment to Hell of Micajah and the disappearance of Wiley, suggest that they were victims of the Harpes rather than aiders and abettors.

One can imagine the trauma suffered by Susan Wood and Betsey Davidson as captives. Very young and completely devoid of the resources necessary to combat the cruel Harpes, they had at first little choice but to placidly accept their fate. Sally Rice, having been seduced in their courtship by the feigned gentility of Wiley Harpe, was eventually put in the same position as the two captives.

All three no doubt suffered from what today is called the battered wife syndrome. Having suffered from psychological and physical abuse they would have blamed themselves for their condition. Unable to assign guilt to their abusers they would have lived in constant fear for their lives and later fear for the lives of their children.

The latter fear was reinforced by Big Harpe, who killed one of their infants and who was at the point of murdering the other two just before being captured and killed. No matter where the women found themselves when they were separated from the Harpe brothers they would have felt that their abusers were always present.

There was no way of escaping from the clutches of the evil brothers until they were finally in their graves.

BIBLIOGRAPHY

Rothert, Otto A. The Outlaws of Cave-In-Rock. Cleveland, 1924.

http://archive.org/details/outlawsofcaveinr00roth

Hall, James. Letters from the West; Containing Sketches of Scenery, Manners, and Customs.

London, 1828. http://archive.org/details/lettersfromwest01hallgoog

Allen, Michael. Western Rivermen, 1763-1861: Ohio and Mississippi Boatmen and the Myth of the Alligator Horse. Louisiana State University Press, 1994.

READY FOR MORE?

We hope you enjoyed reading this series. If you are ready to read similar stories, check out other books in the *Murder and Mayhem* series:

Deadly Darlings: The Horrifying True Accounts of Children Turned Into Murderers (By William Webb)
If you've ever thought your child was bad, then you haven't seen anything yet! In the pages that follow, you are about to meet some of the most vicious children who ever lived.

The kids in this book are as young as ten-years-old and they are ruthless. The nice ones killed in cold blood—but many of these kids weren't nice…they wanted their victims to suffer.

Some were turned killers by their brutal home environments; others were just inherently evil. They were all deadly darlings you'd never want to meet on the street.

The Teacup Poisoner: A Biography of Serial Killer Graham Young (By Fergus Mason)

Graham Young had an unusual obsession from a young age. Where most youths might be interested in music and sports, Young was fascinated by poisons. By the age of 14, he was using his family (who, of course, didn't know) as experiments. In 1962, still a teen, his stepmother died from one of his poisoning experiments.

Young eventually confessed to the murder of his stepmother and the attempted murder of several other members of his family; he was sent to a mental hospital for nine years, where he was ultimately released fully recovered. Unknown to the hospital, however, Young was actually using his time in the mental hospital to study medical texts and improve his poisoning skills. His true work as a poisoner had only just begun!

This gripping narrative gives you a page-turning look at one of England's most notorious serial killers: Graham Young.

The Butcher Baker: The Search for Alaskan Serial Killer Robert Hansen (By Reagan Martin)

Beautiful Alaska--a peaceful, natural land where you know your neighbors and don't have to lock your doors. For most people, it's the perfect place to experience nature; for Robert Hansen, it was the perfect place for murder.

Between 1980 and 1983, Hansen went on a murderous rampage killing between 17 and 37 women in the Anchorage, Alaska area. Hansen, a small-business owner, and pillar of the community was also an avid hunter and used young girls as prey when he decided he needed a more challenging hunt.

This book is the gripping account of the hunt and eventual capture of an unlikely killer, who almost got away with it.

Mary Cecilia Rogers and the Real Life Inspiration of Edgar Allan Poe's Marie Roget (By Wallace Edwards)

The murder of Mary Rogers may not be well known today, but in the 19th century, it was one of the most compelling murders of the century. It became a national sensation--so much so that Edgar Allan Poe used it as the inspiration for his story "The Mystery of Marie Roget."

This chilling narrative will take you back in time to 1838, where you will learn the details of the case and how it became a national phenomenon.

Miscarriage of Justice: The Murder of Teresa de Simone (By Fergus Mason)

The murder was brutal--raped and strangled. The case was open and shut--a man had confessed to the murder, and he was easily convicted. There was a problem with the man's testimony, however...he was a pathological liar who had confessed to over 200 other crimes--many of which never happened.

For over 27 years, Sean Hodgson, the convicted murderer, sat in prison for a crime he didn't commit. The real killer, 17-year-old David Lace, had also confessed to the crime, but police didn't believe him.

This gripping short book takes the reader on the hunt for the real killer and reveals the creation of Operation Iceberg--the operation that led to the DNA review of over 240 other convictions.

No Guns Allowed On Casual Friday: 15 Of the Scariest Co-Workers You Will Never Want to Work With (By William Webb)
Almost everyone thinks it: "One day I'm going to give my boss what he has coming." The fifteen people in this book took this notion to the extreme.

What kind of workplace drives a person into performing such heinous acts? Does a workplace drive a person to kill, or is the killer already inside, waiting for a reason to act out? Find out in this fascinating quick read.

If you are stressed at work, then maybe this book will show you that you don't have it so bad; or maybe it will show you that the person in the cubicle next to you may need to be handled a little more…delicately.

Newsletter Offer

Don't forget to sign up for your newsletter to grab your free book:

http://www.absolutecrime.com/newsletter

Lightning Source UK Ltd.
Milton Keynes UK
UKHW020209031221
395003UK00005B/244